Goods

Ashley Lee

Explore other books at:
WWW.ENGAGEBOOKS.COM

VANCOUVER, B.C.

e→ WWW.ENGAGEBOOKS.COM

Goods: Level 2
I Can Help Save Earth!
Lee, Ashley 1995 –
Text © 2021 Engage Books
Design © 2021 Engage Books

Edited by: A.R. Roumanis

Text set in Arial Regular.
Chapter headings set in Arial Black.

FIRST EDITION / FIRST PRINTING

LIBRARY AND ARCHIVES CANADA CATALOGUING IN PUBLICATION

Title: Goods: I Can Help Save Earth Level 2
Names: Lee, Ashley, 1995- author

Identifiers: Canadiana (print) 2020030982x | Canadiana (ebook) 20200309838
ISBN 978-1-77437-732-1 (hardcover)
ISBN 978-1-77437-733-8 (softcover)
ISBN 978-1-77437-734-5 (pdf)
ISBN 978-1-77437-735-2 (epub)
ISBN 978-1-77437-736-9 (kindle)

Subjects:
LCSH: Consumption (Economics)—Environmental aspects—Juvenile literature
LCSH: Shopping—Environmental aspects—Juvenile literature
LCSH: Environmental protection—Citizen participation—Juvenile literature

Classification: LCC HC79.C6 .L44 20200 | DDC J339.4/7—DC23

Contents

What Are Goods?

Goods are things that people buy. People use goods every day.

Goods can be things you need, like clothes, shoes, or a bed. They can also be things you don't need, but want, like toys or games.

How Are Goods Made?

Some goods are handmade by people in their homes or in small shops. These goods are usually made one at a time.

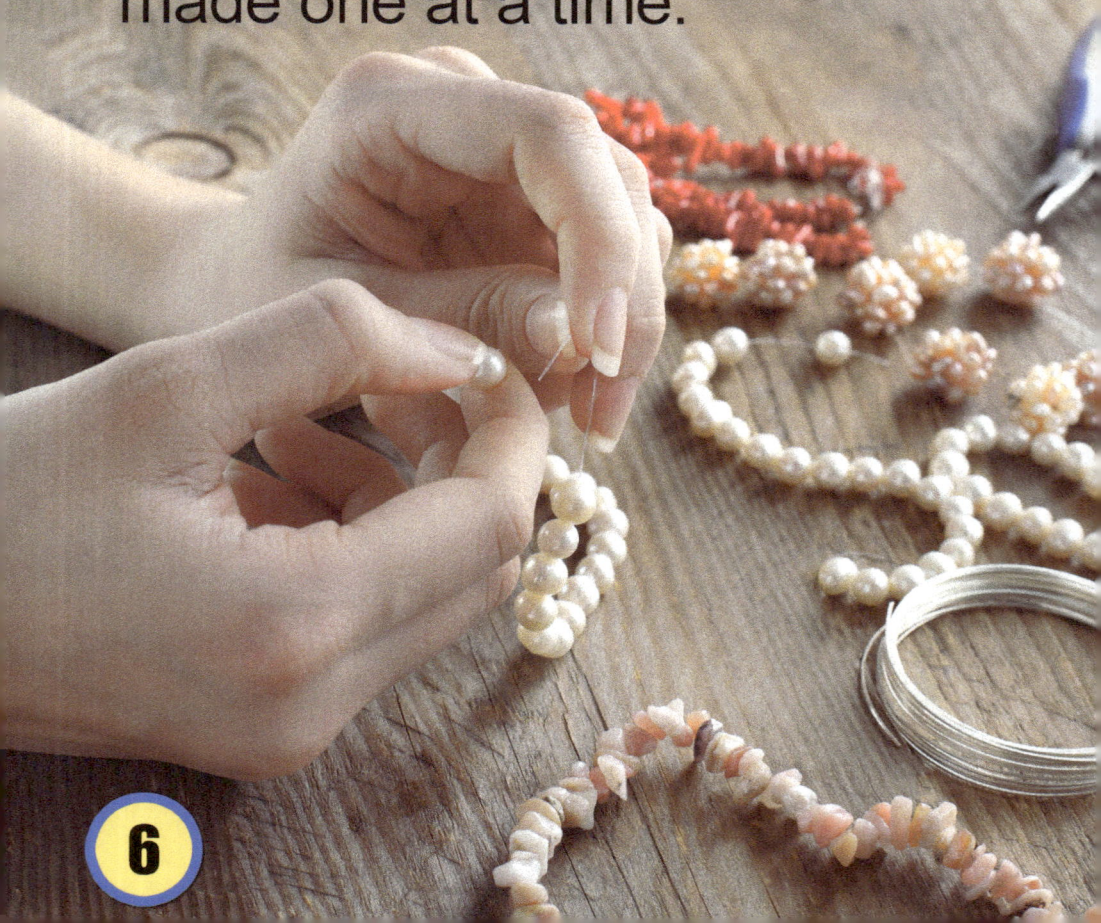

Many goods are made in factories using machines. Factories often make lots of goods at one time.

Why Are Goods Important?

Goods help make people's lives easier. Cars help people travel long distances. Stoves help people make healthy meals.

Medical supplies, toothbrushes, and soap are all goods that help keep people healthy.

9

Goods Around the World

China, the United States, and Japan create more goods than any other countries. They ship their goods to other countries to be sold.

China creates more toys and games than other countries. India is one of the biggest producers of shoes. People in America buy more goods than people in other countries.

Arctic Ocean

North America

China

Asia

Pacific Ocean

America

India

Indian Ocean

Australia

How Do Goods Cause Pollution?

Many goods end up at a landfill. Rain water mixes with the chemicals in goods to create a liquid called leachate. Most leachate is cleaned and released into rivers or oceans. Cleaned leachate can still be harmful to plants and animals.

When landfills become full, they are covered with a layer of plastic and soil. This prevents air from getting to the garbage. As the garbage tries to break down without air, it releases a harmful gas. This gas is one of the causes of **global warming**.

Are All Goods Harmful?

Many goods are made with natural materials like wood. These materials usually break down without releasing harmful chemicals into the soil.

Handmade goods often last longer than goods made in factories. It is easier to make sure goods are well-made when they are made one at a time. Goods that are not well-made end up at the landfill quickly.

Goods Pollution Facts

The United States creates more than 2 billion tons (2.03 billion metric tons) of waste every year.

Around eighty percent of all items buried in landfills could have been recycled.

There are more than 3000 landfills in use in the United States.

16

Between 30 and 300 kinds of animals are forced to move from an area when new landfills are built.

About twenty five percent of waste in American landfills are cardboard or paper products.

Over 11 million tons (11.1 million metric tons) of clothing and shoes end up in landfills every year.

How Goods Pollution Affects Animals

Many animals try to find food at landfills. They sometimes eat pieces of garbage or harmful chemicals. This can make them very sick. Water that contains leachate can also make animals sick.

When one landfill is full, people need to find space for another one. This often means cutting down trees to make space. This destroys animal **habitats**.

How Goods Pollution Affects Humans

Many gases are released from goods breaking down at landfills. This can make people sick.

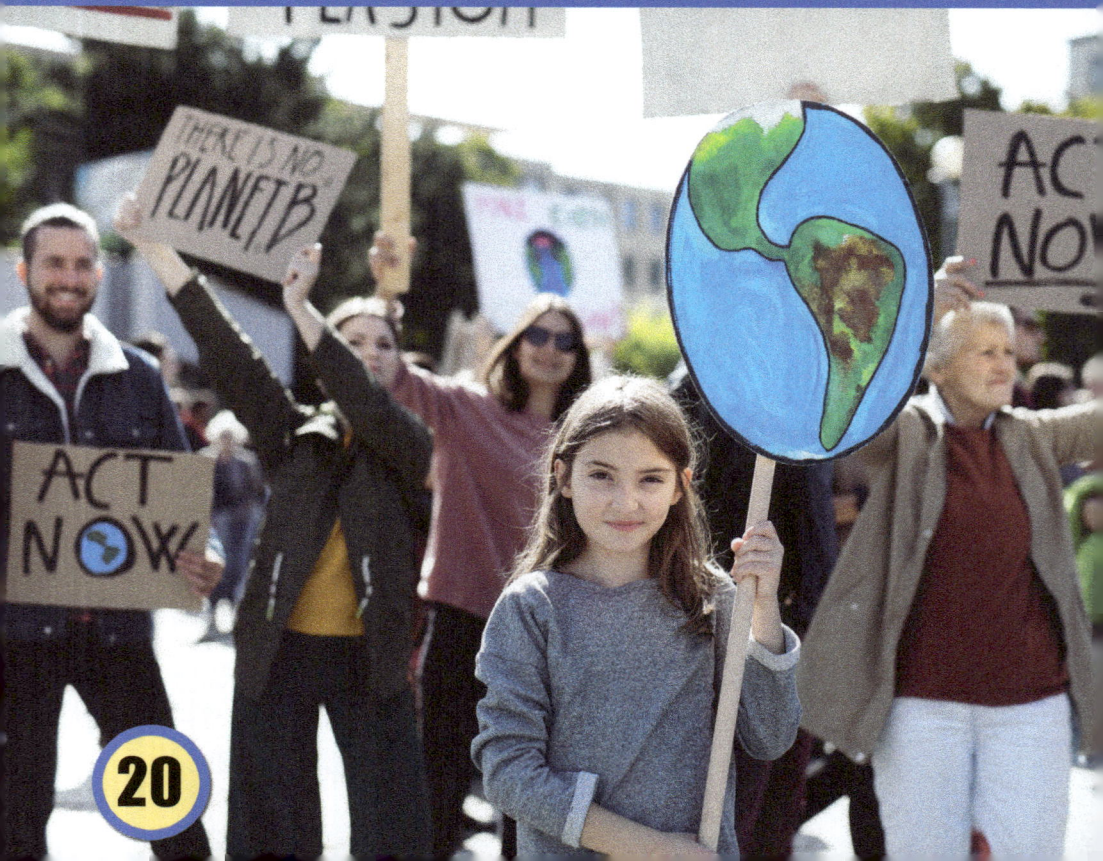

Many countries like Canada and the United States ship large amounts of garbage to other countries. Some towns in the Philippines have piles of garbage on every street. The people who live there are afraid to drink the water since it may contain leachate.

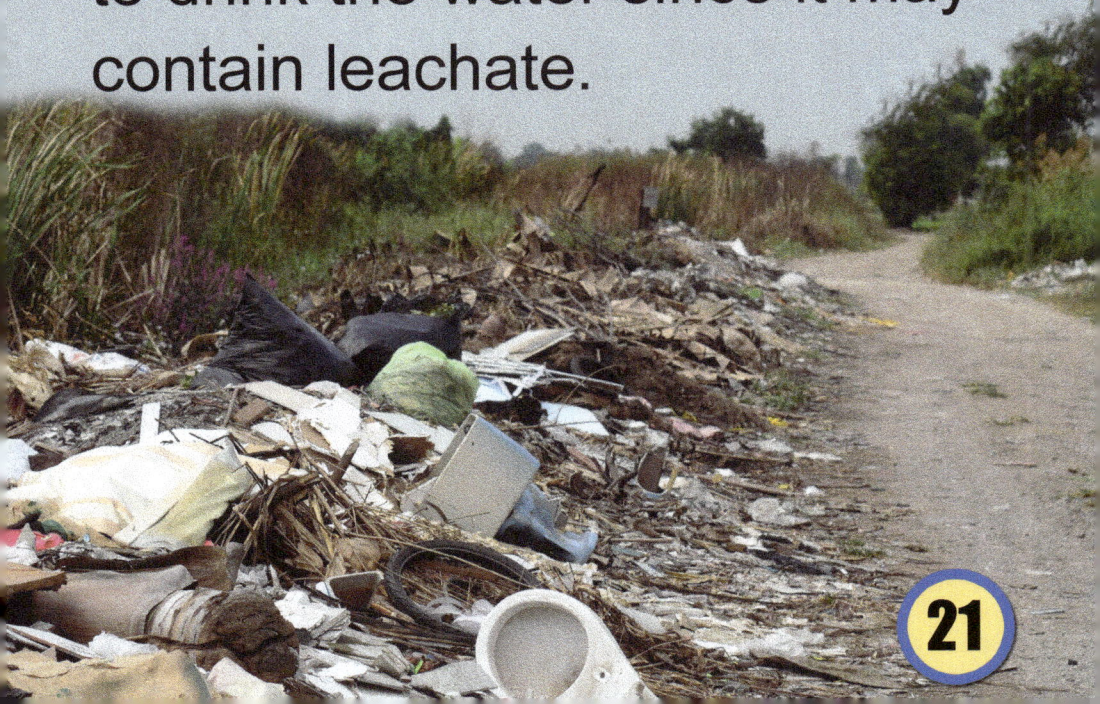

How Goods Pollution Affects Earth

Rising temperatures from global warming is melting ice in Antarctica and the Arctic. As the ice melts, more water is added to the ocean.

Rising oceans cause more dangerous storms like hurricanes and **typhoons**.

KEY WORD

Typhoons: large storms that are formed in a spiral pattern. Typhoons cause strong wind and heavy rain.

Recycling Goods

Recycling means turning an old item into something new. Many kinds of paper and plastic can be recycled. This helps stop landfills from getting full too quickly.

Second-hand stores take used items people no longer want. They sell them to others at a lower price. This helps keep goods out of landfills.

Cleaning Up Goods Pollution

Willow trees are able to absorb chemicals that may harm other plants. Scientists in Canada are using leachate to water fields of willow trees.

Willow trees remove any harmful chemicals from the leachate but keep in any nutrients that will help them grow. This helps keep leachate out of rivers and oceans.

The Future of Goods

Some companies ask customers to return their old televisions, computers, and cellphones. They are able to recycle old parts to make new items.

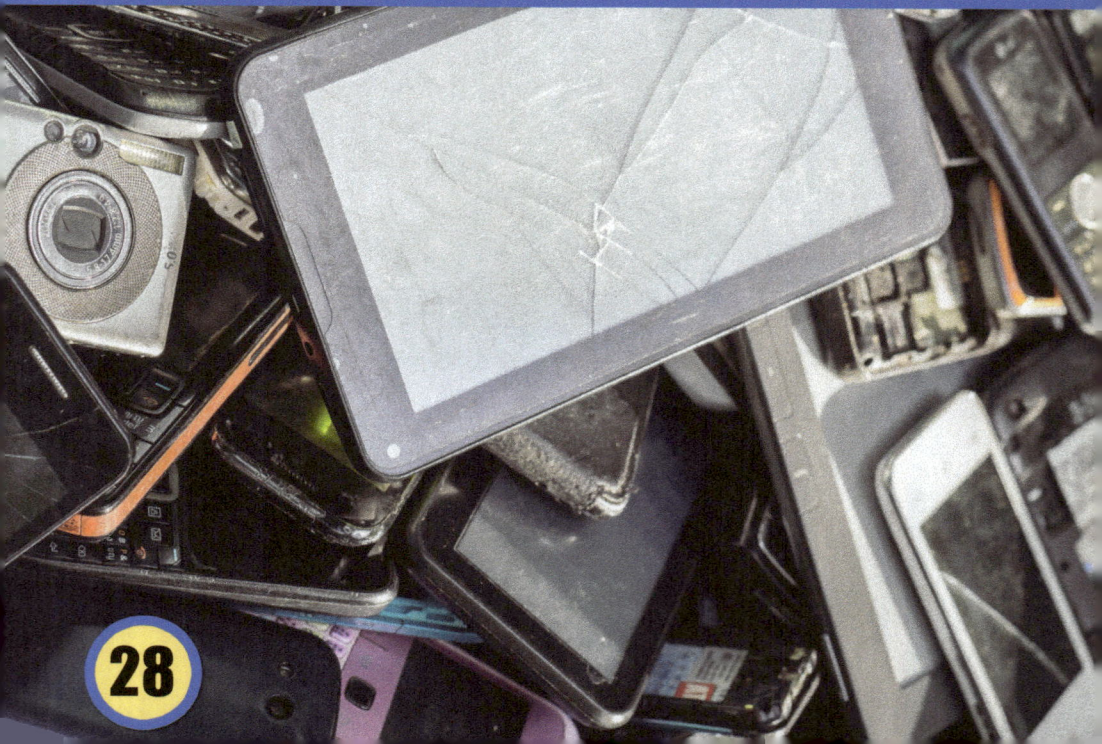

Many people are only buying goods that will last them a long time. They are no longer buying goods that will break easily or can only be used a few times.

Toothbrush   **Electric toothbrush**

Plastic container   **Glass container**

Plastic cup   **Water bottle**

Quiz

Test your knowledge of goods by answering the following questions. The questions are based on what you have read in this book. The answers are listed on the bottom of the next page.

1 What country is one of the largest producers of shoes?

2 What is global warming?

3 What happens to goods that are not well-made?

4 What happens when a landfill is full?

5 What can cause dangerous storms?

6 What are second-hand stores?

Explore other level 2 readers.

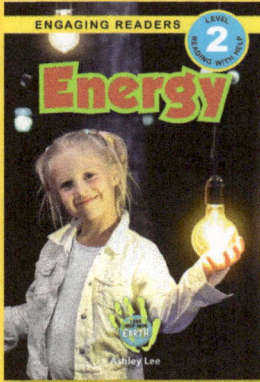

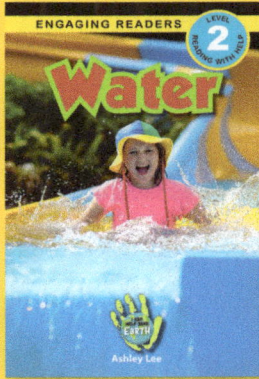

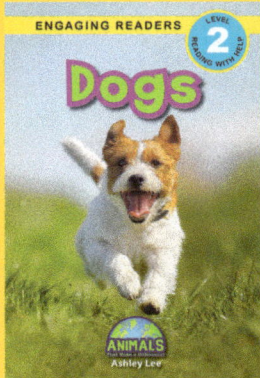

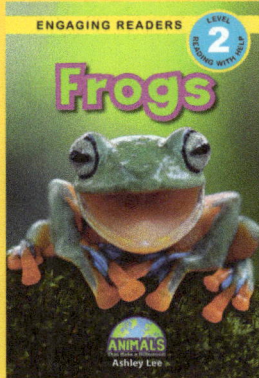

ENGAGING READERS · LEVEL 2 · READING WITH HELP
Energy
Ashley Lee

ENGAGING READERS · LEVEL 2 · READING WITH HELP
Food
Ashley Lee

ENGAGING READERS · LEVEL 2 · READING WITH HELP
Goods
Ashley Lee

ENGAGING READERS · LEVEL 2 · READING WITH HELP
Plastics
Ashley Lee

ENGAGING READERS · LEVEL 2 · READING WITH HELP
Water
Ashley Lee

ENGAGING READERS · LEVEL 2 · READING WITH HELP
Butterflies
Ashley Lee

ENGAGING READERS · LEVEL 2 · READING WITH HELP
Dogs
Ashley Lee

ENGAGING READERS · LEVEL 2 · READING WITH HELP
Frogs
Ashley Lee

ENGAGING READERS · LEVEL 2 · READING WITH HELP
Primates
Ashley Lee

Visit www.engagebooks.com to explore more Engaging Readers.

Answers: 1. India 2. An increase in Earth's temperature 3. They end up at the landfill quickly 4. People need to find space for another one 5. Rising oceans 6. Stores that take used items people no longer want

31